Waltzing
with
GOD

JJ Hammond
with Rae Hight

WESTBOW
P R E S S®
A DIVISION OF THOMAS NELSON
& ZONDERVAN

WestBow Press books may be ordered through booksellers or by contacting:

WestBow Press
A Division of Thomas Nelson & Zondervan
1663 Liberty Drive
Bloomington, IN 47403
www.westbowpress.com
1 (866) 928-1240

ISBN: 978-1-9736-3655-7 (sc)
ISBN: 978-1-9736-3654-0 (hc)
ISBN: 978-1-9736-3656-4 (e)

Library of Congress Control Number: 2018909731

Print information available on the last page.

WestBow Press rev. date: 03/22/2019

To Jesus and His mission to minister to sinners, free them from their transgressions, and restore their hearts so they may follow Him into eternity. This book is also dedicated to those who have sparked my passion for God, Jesus, and the Holy Spirit. Since my walk with Jesus began, my life has been transformed in many ways.

It remains difficult to find the words to describe my journey. The following poems mirror the path I continue to walk to further enrich my relationship with the Holy Trinity. These poems are not mine; they are of God. I am but His scribe.

Contents

Acknowledgments

I am forever grateful to Patty and Daryll Brady. They lit the fire that led me to opening my heart to Jesus and then prayed with and for me. Following this, they introduced me to their home worship center, Crossroads Neighborhood Church.

In 2015, Pastor Gary Tangeman organized an incredible ten-day pilgrimage to the Holy Land. Members of our congregation, as well as other congregations, were included in this once-in-a-lifetime trip. If given the opportunity to travel to Israel, jump on it! You won't regret going.

With the expertise of Miriam, our tour guide, each day was filled with touring historical sites. We were able to visit the Ascension Church, the Northern Wall (once referred to as the Wailing Wall), and the Dead Sea. We also saw one of the locations where Jesus preached. My husband and I were baptized in the Jordan River by Pastor Gary Tangeman. We saw so much more, it is difficult to list them all here.

* * *

Rae Hight—life coach, editor, and therapist—supported me in every aspect of my life. She assisted me in healing wounds that separated me from others and from my God. Thank you, Rae. Your persistence in getting to the heart of my challenges allowed me to grow, making it possible to write this book.

Tom, thank you for your love and devotion. You have held me through all my rough spots. You are my high tower, my soul mate, and I will love you till the end of eternity. Without you in my life striking a path, this journey would be for naught. You saved my life, and I am forever in your debt. You are a gift from God, and I will always cherish our marriage.

* * *

Family

The Girls and Mom

When I was nine years old, I discovered the pleasure of words. I felt the excitement that flowed through me as I wrote my first poem. More than that, I learned how to release the pent-up feelings that held me captive over the years. I discovered how to use words in a way I had never known before. Creativity flourished like a fountain as my siblings and our mother were very creative. In fact, it was our mother who instilled in us the beauty of and love for the arts.

Our mother was a professional pianist who was a remarkable and brave woman. She played evenings Monday through Saturday at nightclubs. She taught piano at home on Saturdays from 10:00 a.m. to 4:00 p.m. Following this, she was out the door on her way to work from 5:00 p.m. to 12:30 a.m. Sundays, she taught piano lessons till noon, then she was able to rest for the remainder of the day. She played in many jazz festivals across the region. My mother attended West Texas State (WTS), where she focused on classical music. Following her time at WTS, she became a self-taught jazz musician.

Yet it was my older twin sisters, Jana and Jill, who left the most impact on me. They became the caretakers, the parents of the four younger children. Jana and Jill lost their high school years taking care of us. While they both had boyfriends, their time with them was limited. They taught us many things, including making a meal and cleaning up afterward. We also learned to do manual labor, such as laundry and cleaning our rooms. From them we also learned kindness toward each other and those outside our home, and trust among ourselves and others.

Jana and Jill were fun, too, creating entertaining activities. One of my favorites was when they turned a mundane dinner into a family restaurant. They designed menus with different entrees for us to choose from. Jana became the waitress, serving our dinners, while Jill was the premier chef. After dinner, it was our task to clean the kitchen.

Still, their lives were not their own; their lives belonged to us. Things changed for them when they graduated from high school. Jana and Jill moved from Kansas to Oklahoma to attend college. I remember the day they left for college. It was both a sad and a thrilling time. Their lives were finally returned to them as they pushed onward, living life for themselves. Today, they both have families and enjoy spending time with each other when their busy lives allow.

Jana and Jill, thank you for all you did for our brothers and myself. We are forever grateful to you. Your kindness and support during those times made a world of difference to us.

***

The Boys and Dad

My brothers—Kelly, Carey, and Chris (twins)—were closest to me in age.

Kelly's belief in God is a soul deep passion that drives his life. He possesses a raw and natural talent that revealed itself at an early age. Kelly first sketched with pencil, pen and charcoal. Soon after, he began painting with oils and acrylics. Mastering painting for the moment, he developed a love for woodworking that continues to this day.

Chris, also a natural artist, had an incredible eye for fine detail. He could connect each line to reproduce in charcoal an accurate picture from any photo. He too enjoyed woodworking and brought his vision to enhance any project, including benches, tables, garden gates and arches. I have always thought of Chris as a true Renaissance man because of his many interests and talents.

Carey is the most innovative of us all. He wasn't a natural artist, but he practiced until his artwork was equal to that of his brothers. Carey was ingenious. Once he took apart our father's alarm clock so it raced around on the floor like a car. He then returned the car to its original shape and function. Carey created a popular board game. He has written several screenplays and is finishing his first novel.

My father was an amazing man with a wonderful sense of humor. In the early 1960s, he shaved my brother's heads and then finished the job by shaving his initials into what little hair they had left. My brothers hated this and made him fix it.

My father was also an excellent artist. Once he painted our kitchen walls with goblets, a variety of fruit, and other kitchen items. Our mother did not like his paintings and made him return our kitchen walls to their original condition. Our father not only put himself through law school, he also put his younger brother and older sister through college as well.

The War We Wage

These times
have found us

wrapped
around a corner,

wrapped
around a heart,

wrapped
around a family.

Still the children play,

no matter
the evening news,

no matter
the wars we wage

nor the God
to whom we pray.

God is wrapped
around these times,

is wrapped around us all.

The War We Wage
Western Wall
Jerusalem, Israel

Profound Faith

He touched each of us through
His grace and mercy.

He bled for humanity.
He died to forgive our sins.

Jesus, I love You.
I hear You call my name.

Profound Faith

Statue of St. Peter
Capernaum, Israel

I Can

I can
feel
His presence
upon me,
His grace within me.

I know He
will always
be with me.

I will never
be alone with Jesus
breathing in my heart.

I Can

Church of Anunciation
Nazareth, Israel

Courageous

are those
who withstand
all the name-calling
to hold true to themselves
through the thunderous
storms they
face each day.

Hold onto
yourself with
heart and grit.

Surrender not
the shield
God
has laid
upon your
soul.

Courageous
Deer in backyard
Kitsap County, Washington

Dancing in the Air

Fingers run against
the edge of being,
racing into another nervous night.

Skies light up,
reflecting
a starry cosmos,
near to heaven.

Dancing in the Air
Night sky in backyard
Kitsap County, Washington

I Remember This Loneliness

It is an echo of a childhood
long lost,
folded and rolled
into numbness,
layered like soil of the earth.

The tears and the pain smeared upon
a small child hiding
in guilt and shame,

knowing all the
while she was to blame
for the monsters and the madness
living inside her house.

Oh, yes, I remember this isolation,
how it suffocated me while the numbness
consumed me whole.

Inside the darkness I felt
the voice of God hold me as He spoke,
"Hush, My child, climb into My arms.
For an eternity I will hold you,
and always I will love you."

At long last, there are no monsters in my house.

I Remember This Loneliness
Paulina Falls
Eastern Oregon

Savior

His spirit encompasses
the whole of the universe.

Jesus, our cherished Savior,
forgives with love and grace.

Hold Him near to your heart.
Praise Him for His blessings,
and pray for those in need.

Savior
Jesus Preached Here.
Jerusalem, Israel

Life Cycles

Bury me among
the trees, sweet Jesus.

Dig the soil rich and deep,
inspire my roots
to grow strong.

Plant me
among the mighty oak
so I may witness
the golden eagle

presenting itself to life
as it ascends beyond
the walls of sky.

Life Cycles
Ancient Pistachio Tree
Tel Dan Park
Tel Dan, Israel

Spirit Never Old

It is
Your
grace
that
forgives
sin,

shedding
new light
upon the depth
of an old soul.

Spirit Never Old
Tel Aviv, Israel

Steps

In a single step
when all is lost,
know that
God is within you,

loving you,
holding space for you,
and releasing you from
your illusions.

Steps
Church of Beatitudes
Capernaum, Israel

Serenity Blooms

Purify the
atmosphere;
make it holy
for Him.

Sanctify the
spirit's design
to take flight
into sacred lives.

Serenity Blooms
Solitary Tree
Oysterville, Washington

Jesus Wore

Jesus wore
His flesh
that day
as He hung
upon the cross.

Jesus bled for
our sins
that day
to set us free
from the inequities
committed against
God and Christ.

I walk with
my Savior today,
and every day is His.

Jesus Wore
Cross
Kitsap County, Washington

Trees

Trees stand still
to salute the skies
and all brave birds.

I sit with them in trees,
touching their essences
with my camera fixed still.

Talking to them,
I toss out seeds
and whisper,
"Thank you."

Together we share
God's majesty.

Trees
Cape Meares Park
Tillamook, Oregon

Connected

As spiritual beings, our power
belongs to God.
Our connectedness with each other
is given to us by God.

We confuse and diffuse our power
when we separate ourselves
from each other and from
God.

Our focus needs to be
connecting with God
and each other,

empowering ourselves as
spirit-filled beings.

Connected
Chapel of Gethsemane
Jerusalem, Israel

Being the Whole

In a single moment,
when we feel His presence
drawing us to His grace,
all is possible—

forgiveness, love,
being the whole.

He saw in each of us
our essence,

who we would become
as He spoke our names;
the thumbprint of God
whispered inside each soul.

Being the Whole
Jesus Praying
Garden of Gethsemane
Jerusalem, Israel

Spirit of God

Should hate or disdain
fester in your heart,

there remains no room
for God.

If you cannot,

will not

forgive another,

how is God
to forgive
you?

Spirit of God
Weathered Door
Eastern Washington

Breakfast with Jesus

I am the pilot
of my dreams.
I soar through
blue sky and over
mountaintops.

I rise to sit
with Jesus
every morning.

He is my Lord,
the pilot
of my heart,
the keeper
of my soul.

Breakfast with Jesus
Autumn moon over trees
Kitsap County, Washington

God's Garden

It is to Jesus alone
I reveal myself.
I bloom before Him
completely and freely

till finally,
I unfold
and reflect
on the faith
I hold for Him.

God's Garden
Garden of Gethsemane
Jerusalem, Israel

Let Not Your Hatred

Let not your hatred
become your poison,
nor your anger
creep into cancer.

Remember God.

Recall the seeds
He's planted,
the grace
He's granted
for you and for me.

Lose not your way
and fail to see
the eyes of God
looking at you
through those
you choose
to hate.

Let Not Your Hatred

Byzantine Cross at a baptismal site
Bet She'an, Israel

Passions of Life

How would you
spread the colors
you weave?

In what way would you
paint upon your canvas?

Have you spent time
in grateful prayer
with the presence
of God close by?

What are the words
that soothe your soul,
releasing all that
God holds for you?

Passions of Life
Wilderness Frontier
Alaska

I Have Lost

I have lost

my way before,

misplaced my steps.

Yet I have never lost

sight of my God.

He reigns in my heart

and dwells within my soul.

I Have Lost
Illuminated Sky
Kitsap County, Washington

In All We Press

In all we press
there is God.

His essence finds its way
into our beings,
gives birth
to our spirits, and
speaks to us
softly, loudly,
and directly.

God hears our thoughts;
He is in the next thought
and the next.

Where do your thoughts dwell?

In All We Press
Hiking Trail
Pacific Northwest

This Then Is Your Gift

This then is your gift,
the gift God
did not loan you.

The gift God
placed inside
your soul,

waiting for the moment
when you reach inside
and untie its bow.

This Then is Your Gift

Garden of Gethsemane
Jerusalem, Israel

Powerful

Grace
holds its
beauty

sealed with
His
truth

and
bonded by

His power
of love.

Powerful

Carmelite Monastery
Haifa, Israel

My God's Creation

In God's
palette of colors,
reflecting all of
man- and womankind,

how joyous
was He
when His creations
were complete.

Colors sail
across the
vast horizon
of all
humankind.

Bow unto
the sacredness
of the

palette of
God's colors.

My God's Creation
Church of Ascension
Jerusalem, Israel

I See Your Sunset

unfold before me
as I witness
Your glory.

I feel You
breathe deeply
inside my soul
with all Your passion

so tender,
so bold.

To You I offer
every beat
of my
heart.

To You I promise
all the steps
I call my own.

It is with You
I rest,
and it is with You

I call my home.

I See Your Sunset

Theler Wetlands
Belfair, Washington

I See the Poetry

I see the poetry
of God's grandeur
upon the faces of
young and old.

God's wisdom
fills our lives,
leaving nothing
in our hearts
but His love.

I See the Poetry
Wood Sculpture Weathered by the Ocean
Washington State

All I Ever Hoped For

All I ever hoped for
was peace between us.

In the absence of this peace,
all that remains

are pieces
between us all.

All I Ever Hoped For

Man in Clouds with Heaven Rays
Kitsap County, Washington

In My Father's Eyes

God dwells in every
breath we take—
the drawing in,
the letting go.

He calls attention
to our inner beauty,
unfolding in
every moment
of every day.

He teaches us to
be more compassionate
with those in need.

Extend God's love;
be slow to offer
an unkind heart.

In My Father's Eyes
Lake Wenatchee, Washington

Solstice

Peace

rolled

brilliantly

off the

cliffs of

humanity

into the

the arms of

God.

Solstice

Fort Rock
High Desert, Oregon

We Know Him as Jesus

He breathes
in us all.
He lives
in our
footsteps.

He inspires
the quality
of the lives
Christians believe.

He expands
our souls,
whispers
into our
hearts and minds.

We know Him as Jesus.

We Know Him as Jesus

Baptism in the Jordan River
with Pastor Gary E. Tangeman
Jerusalem, Israel

Harmony of God

God, bless our country
and our skies.

God, protect the
good air we breathe.

God, shield all the
wonders of our land.

Father, thank You for the
preciousness of life.

Harmony of God
Neighbor's Yard
Kitsap County, Washington

Too Much Time

Too much time has passed
by my window
to dwell upon
what others may think,

judging my steps
or the way
I dance in the streets
of my life.

God took care in
designing us,
loving us
as only He can.

We are hidden treasures
created
for each other,
revealing
His love through us.

Too Much Time
Front Yard
Kitsap County, Washington

Nurture Your Dreams

Yours are the dreams
given you,
authored by God.

Nurture their essence,
your treasures to reap.

Nurture Your Dreams
Denali National Park
Matanuska-Susitna Borough, Alaska

Notes

Notes

Notes

Notes

Notes

Notes

Notes

Notes

Notes

Notes

Notes

Notes

Notes

Notes

Notes

Notes

Notes

Notes

Notes

Notes

Notes

Notes

CPSIA information can be obtained
at www.ICGtesting.com
Printed in the USA
BVHW030801190419
545923BV00010B/9/P

9 781973 636540